CONTINENTS

South America

Mary Virginia Fox

Heinemann
LIBRARY

www.heinemann.co.uk/library
Visit our website to find out more information about Heinemann Library books.

To order:
☎ Phone 44 (0) 1865 888066
Send a fax to 44 (0) 1865 314091
Visit the Heinemann Bookshop at www.heinemann.co.uk/library to browse our
catalogue and order online.

First published in Great Britain by Heinemann Library, Halley Court, Jordan Hill, Oxford OX2 8EJ, part of Harcourt Education. Heinemann is a registered trademark of Harcourt Education Ltd.

Editorial: Kathy Peltan, Clare Lewis, and Katie Shepherd
Design: Joanna Hinton-Malivoire and Q2A Creative
Picture research: Erica Newbery
Production: Helen McCreath

Origination: Modern Age Repro House Ltd.
Printed and bound in China by South China Printing Co. Ltd.

10-digit ISBN 0-431-15810-X
13-digit ISBN 978-0-431-15810-5
10 09 08 07 06
10 9 8 7 6 5 4 3 2 1

British Library Cataloguing in Publication Data
Fox, Mary Virginia
South America. – 2nd ed. – (Continents)
918
A full catalogue record for this book is available from the British Library.

Acknowledgements
The publishers would like to thank the following for permission to reproduce photographs: Earth Scenes/Fabio Colonbini, p. **5**; Photo Edit/E. Zuckerman, p. **6**; Earth Scenes/Breck P. Kent, pp. **9**, **19**; Tony Stone/Kevin Schafer, p. **11**; Corbis/Adam Woolfitt, p. **13**; Brian Vikander, p. **14**; Animals Animals/Partridge, p. **15**; Earth Scenes, p. **16**; DDB Stock Photo/ Robert Fried, p. **21**; Tony Stone/Avenida Paulista, p. **22**; Peter Arnold/Jeff Greenberg, Inc., p. **23**; Earth Scenes/Nigel J. H. Smith, p. **24**; Earth Scenes/Michael Fogden, p. **25**; Bruce Coleman/Timothy O'Keefe, Inc., p. **27**; Tony Stone/Ary Diesendruck, p. **28**; Photo Researchers/Georg Gerster, p. **29**.

Cover photograph of South America, reproduced with permission of Science Photo Library/ Tom Van Sant, Geosphere Project/ Planetary Visions.

The publishers would like to thank Kathy Peltan and Nancy Harris for their assistance in the preparation of this book.

Every effort has been made to contact copyright holders of any material reproduced in this book. Any omissions will be rectified in subsequent printings if notice is given to the publishers.

The paper used to print this book comes from sustainable resources.

Some words are shown in bold, **like this**. You can find out what they mean by looking in the glossary.

Contents

Where is South America?

A continent is a very large area of land. There are seven continents in the world. South America is one of them. A narrow strip of land connects South America to the continent of North America.

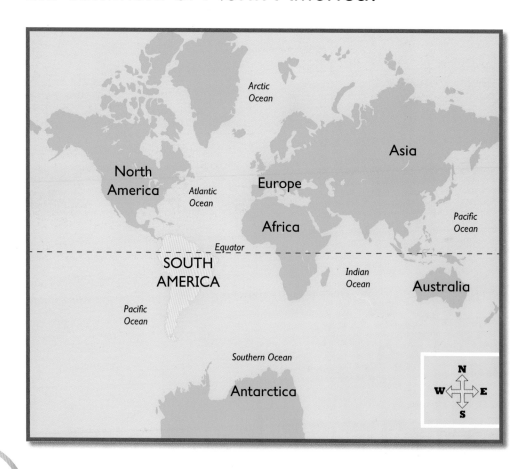

▲ *Sandy beach on Brazil's Atlantic coast*

South America is almost completely surrounded by oceans. The Pacific Ocean is to the west. The Atlantic Ocean is to the east. Most of South America is below the **Equator**. The Equator is an imaginary line around the centre of the Earth.

Weather

The **Equator** crosses South America near its widest part. Here, there are **tropical rainforests**. The weather is hot and rainy all year. There are grasslands north and south of the rainforest. It is hot and mainly dry there.

South America has the world's largest rainforest.

▲ *Amazon River winding through the rainforest*

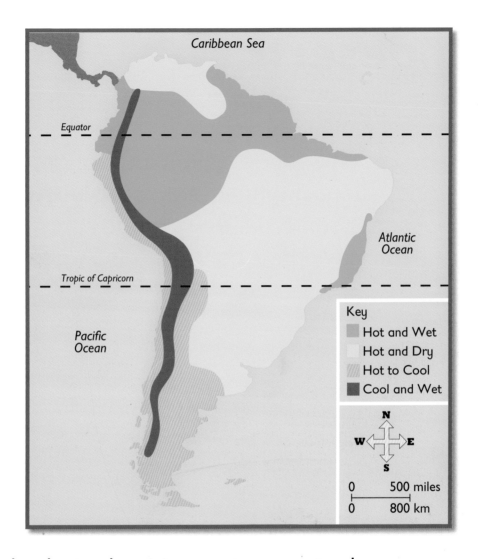

The high Andes Mountains are in the west of South America. They have cool and rainy weather. It is very cold and windy at the southern tip of South America.

Mountains and deserts

The Andes mountain **range** is in South America. It is the longest mountain range in the world. There are hundreds of **volcanoes** in the Andes. Some still **erupt** today. The tallest peak is Mount Aconcagua in Argentina.

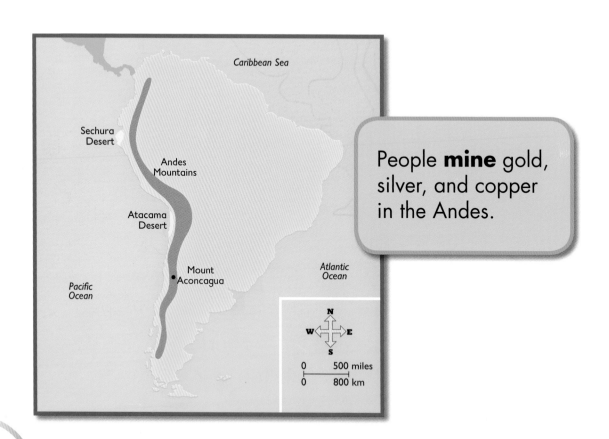

People **mine** gold, silver, and copper in the Andes.

No rain has ever been recorded in parts of the Atacama Desert.

▲ *The rocky Atacama Desert in Peru*

There are **deserts** on the west coast of South America. It never rains there. During the day, the temperature in these deserts can reach 50°C (122°F). But at night it is bitterly cold.

Rivers

The Amazon is the second longest river in the world. It carries more water than any other river. It begins in an icy lake in the Andes Mountains. Then it flows through dense **rainforest** to the Atlantic Ocean.

Angel Falls is the tallest waterfall in the world.

▲ *Angel Falls, in Venezuela*

Angel Falls is in Venezuela. It is a very tall waterfall. Water falls into a deep **gorge**. People use the energy from the water to create electricity.

Lakes

Caribbean Sea
Lake Guatavita
Lake Titicaca
Lake Poopó
Pacific Ocean
Lake Chiquita
Lake Mirim
Atlantic Ocean
Lake Buenos Aires
N
W
E
S
0
500 miles
0
800 km

South America has many large lakes. Lake Titicaca is high in the Andes Mountains. Giant frogs live among the **reeds** at the edge. People make boats from the reeds and go fishing on the lake.

Lake Guatavita is also in the Andes. Many years ago, people believed that the sun was born here. Before a new **ruler** was crowned, he had to sail to the centre of the lake. He had to throw golden gifts to the gods in the water.

▲ *Lake Guatavita, in the Andes, Colombia*

Animals

High in the mountains, farmers keep llamas, vicuñas, and alpacas. These strong animals look like small camels. They provide milk and meat. Their **dung** is burnt as fuel. People make their long, fine wool into clothes.

▲ *Alpacas carrying grass in Peru*

An anaconda can open its jaws wide enough to eat a whole goat.

▲ *Anaconda searching for prey*

Thousands of creatures live in South America's **rainforests**. Parrots and monkeys live in the trees. Anacondas are one of the world's largest types of snake. They wait in rivers to pounce on their **prey**.

Plants

▲ Sap from a rubber tree

Hundreds of products come from the trees and plants of South America. Rubber is made from the **sap** of rubber trees. Chewing gum is made from another tree. Many medicines have been made from South American plants.

Chocolate is made from the seeds of the cacao tree. Cacao trees grow wild in the **rainforests**. Today cacao is often grown on farms.

The people of South America were the first people to make chocolate.

▲ *Cacao trees in Brazil*

Languages

This map shows the countries in South America. Most people in these countries speak Spanish or Portuguese. Around 500 years ago, explorers came from Spain and Portugal to live in South America.

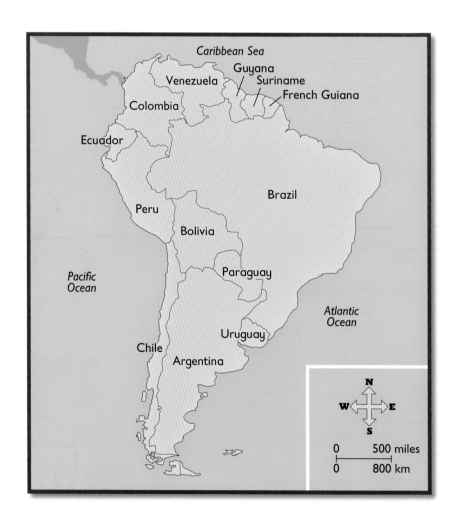

▲ *Yahua people from Peru*

The first people to live in South America were **Native Americans**. They had their own languages and traditions. The Yahua people in Peru still speak their own language.

Cities

This map shows the main cities of South America. Rio de Janeiro is in Brazil. It is the busiest **port** in South America. Rio is famous for its beautiful beaches and lively **festivals**.

Santiago is a beautiful city. It is the **capital** of Chile. It was built by Spanish **settlers** near the Andes Mountains. The people of Santiago made money from **mining** silver and copper.

▲ *Santiago, Chile*

São Paulo is the largest city in South America.

▲ *São Paulo, Brazil*

São Paulo is a busy **port** on the southeast coast. It is also an important centre for buying and selling coffee. São Paulo has many factories that make steel, chemicals, and televisions.

Quito is one of the highest cities in the world.

▲ Quito, Ecuador

Quito is built on the side of a **volcano**. It is the capital of Ecuador. Quito is one of the oldest cities in South America. About 500 years ago, it was the **capital** of an ancient kingdom ruled by the Inca people.

In the country

In the **rainforests** of South America, most people live on rivers. Today, their way of life is in danger. Many trees are being cut down for **timber**, or to clear land for farming.

The easiest way to get from one village to another is to travel by boat.

▲ *Houses on stilts by the Amazon River*

▲ *House built from clay, Peru*

Houses with thick clay walls keep **herders** warm in the cold mountains. Near the rainforest, farmers grow coffee, cacao, and sugar beet. In the cooler south, people grow wheat. There are huge cattle ranches.

Famous places

Tierra del Fuego is a group of rocky islands at the tip of South America. Its name means "land of fire" in Spanish. This is because explorers saw camp fires on the islands. Tierra del Fuego is now a **national park** with penguins and seals.

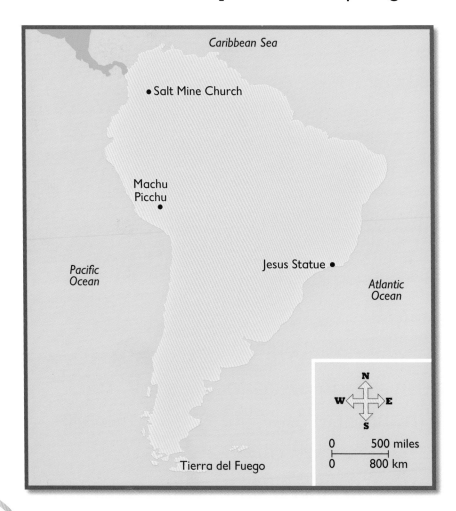

The Inca people built this walled city over 500 years ago.

▲ Machu Picchu, Peru

Machu Picchu is in the Andes Mountains. It stayed hidden from the rest of the world for hundreds of years. The city contained houses, palaces, and **temples**. There was also an observatory, where people could study the stars.

This statue is lit up at night. It can be seen from many miles away.

▲ *Rio de Janeiro, Brazil*

In Rio de Janeiro, a giant statue of Jesus looks down on the harbour. Many people in South America are **Christians**. The Spanish and Portuguese **settlers** built churches and cathedrals all over the continent.

Many people work in **mines** in South America. In Chile, miners dig up copper. In Peru they mine silver. Gold, emerald, and salt are all mined in Colombia.

Even the statues in this church are carved from salt.

▲ *Church carved from a salt mine in Colombia*

Fast facts

South America's longest rivers

Name of river	Length in Kilometres	Length in miles	Countries	Ends
Amazon	6,437	4,000	Peru, Colombia, Brazil	Atlantic Ocean
Parana	3,998	2,484	Brazil, Argentina Paraguay	Atlantic Ocean
Purus	3,379	2,100	Brazil, Peru	Amazon River
Madeira	3,239	2,013	Brazil	Amazon River

Highest mountains in South America

Name of mountain	Height in metres	Height in feet	Country
Aconcagua	6,962	22,841	Argentina
Ojos del Salado	6,880	22,572	Chile
Bonete	6,872	22,545	Argentina
Mercedario	6,770	22,211	Argentina, Chile
Huascaran	6,768	22,204	Peru

South American record breakers

South America's Amazon **rainforest** is the largest in the world.

The Amazon rainforest has more types of plant than any other forest in the world.

The Andes Mountains are the longest mountain **range** in the world. They stretch for over 7,200 kilometres.

The Atacama **Desert** in Chile and Peru is one of the driest places in the world.

Angel Falls in Venezuela has a longer drop than any other waterfall in the world. The water falls for 979 metres (3212 feet).

Glossary

capital city where government leaders work

Christians people who follow the religion of Christianity

desert hot, dry land with little rain

dung droppings of large animals, such as horses or llamas

Equator imaginary circle around the exact middle of the earth

erupt to throw out rocks and hot ash

festival a time when people celebrate something

gorge very deep river valley with steep, rocky sides

herder someone who looks after a group of animals

mine to dig up things from under the earth's surface

national park area of wild land protected by the government

Native Americans first people to live in North and South America

port town or city with a harbour, where ships come and go

prey animal that is eaten by other animals

rainforest thick forest that has heavy rain all year round

range line of mountains that are connected to each other

reeds type of tall grass

ruler person who rules a country, such as a queen or president

sap liquid from a plant or tree

settlers people who come to live in a country

temple place built to worship a god or goddess

timber cut up wood used for making things

tropical hot, wet places near the Equator

volcano hole in the earth from which hot, melted rock is thrown out

More books to read

My World of Geography: Rivers, Angela Royston
(Heinemann Library, 2004)

Watching Tree Frogs in South America, Elizabeth Miles
(Heinemann Library, 2006)

We're from Brazil, Emma Lynch
(Heinemann Library, 2005)

Index